Robert Lowell

Robert Lowell

A LECTURE DELIVERED AT THE
LIBRARY OF CONGRESS
ON MAY 2, 1983

by Anthony Hecht

WASHINGTON
LIBRARY OF CONGRESS
1983

"Sir Thomas More," from *Notebook 1967–68* (New York: Farrar, Straus and Giroux, 1969). Copyright © 1967, 1968, 1969 by Robert Lowell. "Sir Thomas More," from *History* (New York: Farrar, Straus and Giroux, 1973). Copyright © 1967, 1968, 1969, 1970, 1973 by Robert Lowell. "No Hearing," from *Selected Poems* (New York: Farrar, Straus and Giroux, 1977). Copyright © 1967, 1968, 1969, 1970, 1973, 1977 by Robert Lowell. Reprinted by permission of Farrar, Straus and Giroux, Inc.

Frontispiece: Robert Lowell, October 31, 1960.

Library of Congress Cataloging in Publication Data

Hecht, Anthony, 1923–
   Robert Lowell: a lecture delivered at the Library of Congress on May 2, 1983.

   1. Lowell, Robert, 1917–1977—Addresses, essays, lectures. 2. Poets, American—20th century—Biography—Addresses, essays, lectures.   I. Library of Congress. II. Title.
PS3523.O89Z69   1983   811'.52 [B]   83-18781
ISBN 0-8444-0439-X

Available from the Library of Congress, Manuscript Division, Washington, D.C. 20540

Everything is real until it's published.
"Flight to New York"

Robert Lowell

If we may assert with confidence so very soon after his death that Robert Lowell has attained the stature of a major American poet, it is important that we guard against making the claim for any of the wrong reasons. The difficulty arises out of the easy confusion of celebrity with achievement. On the whole, it's easier for fiction writers than for poets to become celebrities: their works can be filmed and televised; because they write prose, it is assumed by talk-show impresarios that they can probably talk; and then celebrity must furnish its own appetite for further celebrity, all of it benignly regarded by promoters and publishers and the public. Poets, on the other hand, though they may be regarded as ipso facto "strange," "passing strange," are only thought interesting if they have a conspicuous vice to exploit or some aggrandizing aberration. And Lowell has undeniably been noticed for lots of reasons that are incidental, if at all related, to his literary attainments. Some have been impressed with the distinction of his family, his ancestral ties to Jonathan Edwards, to the early Pilgrim fathers, as well as to Harvard presidents, and an ambassador to the court of St. James. Some knew he was important because his mental crack-ups received such notoriety; some knew him in terms of the political stances he took, often impetuously and courageously, beginning with his objection to this country's role in World War II and continuing to the protests against our role in Vietnam. Finally, there is the undisputed fact that so soon after his death his biography has been written by the British poet, Ian Hamilton: a certification of Lowell's clear importance, if one were needed. But it should be said that while none of these considerations is trivial or beside the point, they bear only indirectly on Lowell's singular accomplishments. Lowell himself made rather a mockery of the distinction of his family and seems to have felt it rather an encumbrance than anything else. He was frequently appalled by his mental disturbances and by their consequences. His political stances were always taken with seriousness and integrity and never simply in order to get his name or face into print. And this biographer, in distinct contrast with those of certain other modern writers whose weather eyes were cocked for the attention of posterity, was not officially appointed by him.

Lowell's biography was greeted with what may fairly be called rave reviews by Helen Vendler in the leading article in the *New York Review of Books;* by Richard Ellmann on the front page of the *New York Times Book Review;* and by Stephen Spender on the front page of *The Washington Post*'s *Book World*. There is in this a rather poignant irony that is not likely to be lost on Mr. Hamilton, who is himself a poet. Of all the work of a lifetime dedicated to poetry, and abundant in its production, the only volume of Lowell's to receive front page notice in the *Times Book Review* was his last, *Day by Day*, reviewed there admiringly by Helen Vendler on August 14, 1977, less than a month before Lowell's death on September 12. Hamilton's book bids fair to be something of a best-seller and is firmly a book club selection; and, like the reviewers who are on record in praising it, I wish it every success. But he and I will not be alone in imagining that this book will be devoured by many who have no interest in poetry and scarcely any knowledge of Robert Lowell's work.

The sort of prurience that is bound to contribute to the public's interest can be illustrated by an anecdote, true in its major outlines, and from which I have merely deleted the proper names. Some years ago, when Lowell was a firmly acknowledged celebrity, the editors of a "popular" magazine invited one of New York's leading intellectuals, a critic-author-editor of impeccable credentials, to lunch at one of the city's best restaurants to discuss some sort of possible article about the poet. The distinguished critic was intrigued by the emergence of this proposal from so unlikely a source and perhaps engaged by the excellence of the restaurant. It was during the second, soothing martini that the editors began to make clear what it was they hoped the projected article would cover: they wanted to have as much in the way of particulars as could be managed about (a) Lowell's girl friends and extramarital affairs, and (b) his episodes of violence and incarceration in mental hospitals. The critic listened silently, savoring his drink, as these guidelines were laid out for him, and when they seemed to be quite through he asked the editors, "And how much space do you think should be devoted to the *poetry?*" The answer he received convinced him that, of their kind, these were real pros he was dealing with. "Roughly eighty percent of our readership," he was told, "hold B.A.'s, and of those perhaps twenty percent have more advanced degrees. So I think you can safely assume that they will *know* the poetry, and you won't have to bother with it."

And indeed the biography, though sparing in both numbers and details (not a few women will doubtless be outraged to find their names omitted from the chronicle) makes it clear that Lowell's manic cycles almost always involved episodes of sexual adventurism. So much was this the case that at one time his New York psychiatrist, a woman, convinced that somehow Lowell's wife, Elizabeth Hardwick, had a deleterious effect upon the poet, and needed to be kept from him at all costs, nevertheless found herself so mystified by the urgency with which Lowell spoke of someone he was newly obsessed with (or so goes the story as I heard it) that, for all the therapist's hostility to Miss Hardwick, she phoned her to ask, "Who is this Gerta he talks about now all the time?" Miss Hardwick replied truthfully that her husband was talking about the author of *Faust*.

Hamilton's book deserves praise for many things, but I think chiefly for being astonishingly fair to all the major figures in the story he has set out to tell—not in itself an easy task, given a tale so congested with pain and cruelty, infidelity, wildness, and violence—but he is also to be congratulated on his usually respectful and intelligent dealings with the poetry, though he sometimes lapses into unfortunate generalizations and crude conjectures, as shall appear. But he is very keen, subtle, and knowing, for example, about Lowell's poem "Home After Three Months Away," indicating with great care the stratified, geological layers of reference that work down through the poet's entire biography. He is even more helpful, and helped in his turn by the painter Sidney Nolan, in the unraveling of an all but impenetrable poem, "The Misanthrope and the Painter," which seems defiantly hermetic and private. (It's impossible to tell whether the poem was meant to be cryptic, reserved for the understanding of the initiate, or was not sufficiently worked out.) And if Hamilton is sometimes hasty or careless in his dealings with the poetry, it must be added that in the portraiture of his subject he has somehow contrived to omit or gloss over some of Lowell's most endearing characteristics, especially his animated sense of fun and his lively pleasure in the humor of others. Some of his taunting letters—to Peter Taylor, for example—were written in the spirit of outrageous jest and are retailed in this book with a straight face, and without any indication that they could mean anything but what they seem literally to say. But in his honest dealings with his large cast of characters, and in his valuable comments on the poetry, Hamilton has done, I think, rather greater justice to Lowell than has been done to Byron by most of his biographers, some of whom, like Peter Quennell and Harold Nicholson, appear not really to be interested in the poetry at all.

The Byron comparison, while not to be pursued with Euclidean precision, and not Hamilton's but mine, is a fair one in some respects. Both poets were public figures and involved in the political events of their time; both were capable of devastating expressions of scorn for their opponents; both were powerful and handsome men; both were crippled, each in his own way; both were astonishingly attractive to women; both were aristocrats by inheritance (somewhat shabby aristocrats) and democrats by generous instinct; both were the subject of scandalous gossip during and after their lifetimes; and both were poets of acknowledged international stature who *found themselves famous* quite early in life. It may be added that both were bedeviled by strict and relentlessly Puritan consciences and Calvinistic anguish. Hamilton reports that Lowell's nickname, Cal, was meant to stand for Caligula (as Lowell himself acknowledges in a poem) and Caliban. Robie Macauley has told me that it also stood for the Calvin in Calvin Coolidge. While there was something strikingly Julio-Claudian about Lowell's huge head, the Calvin of Geneva, a dim but satanic presence in the poem called "Children of Light" ("Pilgrims unhouseled by Geneva's night, / They planted here the Serpent's seeds of light; . . ."), has, I think, a legitimate part to play in the poet's psychic genealogy.

The nickname of the mad emperor was curiously prophetic because it was assigned to, and adopted by, Lowell before his madness had yet exhibited itself in any forms graver than eccentric recklessness and untidiness. Later, of course, the news of his periodic breakdowns spread with amazing speed, penetrating without difficulty to even the most remote recesses of the world. News, for example, of his Salzburg collapse reached me somehow in provincial Ischia, and I remember passing it on to Auden, expecting from him some grunt of commiseration, at the very least. I could not have been more astonished by his response. He regarded Lowell's whole tortured history of crack-ups as pure self-indulgence and undeserving of any sympathy. It took me many years to come to even a partial understanding of this chilling reaction, and I can only guess that it may have been due to Auden's medical fascination with Georg Groddeck, Homer Lane, and other psychosomatic theorists who believed that virtually all illnesses are *willed*, as well as to a parental inheritance of clinical detachment, and the fact that there was no history of madness in his immediate experience. In fairness it should be added that he may have been at least partly right: Hamilton quotes Jonathan Raban's account of the dolphin binge (the buying of little glass or plaster dolphins) Lowell went on during the writing of *The Dolphin*, a binge that clearly represented a huge exertion of will power directed towards avoiding a crack-up ("So the obsession," Raban reports, "was with dolphins—it never got into great men. Which was a triumph."), and which, in this lone instance, worked. But Auden's lofty, condemnatory tone was to exhibit itself again when Lowell later, in *The Dolphin*, published poems of unprecedented intimacy, with details and even language frankly rifled from private conversations and correspondence, chiefly with his abandoned wife, Elizabeth Hardwick, but with others, like Allen Tate, as well. Hamilton quotes from a letter to Lowell by William Alfred, who had just met Auden for the first time: "He spoke of not speaking to you because of the book. When I said he sounded like God the Father, he gave me a tight smile. I write to warn you." Alas, in both these cases Auden sounds less like the Ancient of Days than like a prim English nanny with a rigid sense of decorum. In fact, Auden is permitted to voice his objections in one of the book's sonnets, called, with some point, "Truth":

> The scouring voice of 1930 Oxford,
> "Nothing pushing the personal should be published,
> not even Proust's *Research* or Shakespeare's *Sonnets,*
> a banquet of raw ingredients in bad taste. . . ."

Undeniably, as Lowell's best and most admiring friends forced themselves to point out to him before publication, the book would be excruciatingly painful to Elizabeth Hardwick. In this regard Elizabeth Bishop wrote Lowell an agonizing letter, urging him not to publish the book, and saying: "... *art just isn't worth that much.*" And Stanley Kunitz must have raised objections no less strong and direct, as he indicated in a memoir published in the October 16, 1977, *New York Times Book Review*, because Lowell wrote to him as follows:

> About your criticism. I expect to be back in New York for a week beginning the 21st of May, and hope to unwind over drinks with you. Dolphin is somewhat changed with the help of Elizabeth Bishop. The long birth sequence will come before the Flight to New York, a stronger conclusion, and one oddly softening the effect by giving a reason other than new love for my departure. Most of the letter poems—E. B.'s objection they were part fiction offered as truth—can go back to your old plan, a mixture of my voice, and another voice in my head, part me, part Lizzie, italicized, paraphrased, imperfectly, obsessively heard. I take it, it is these parts that repel you. I tried the new version on Peter Taylor, and he couldn't imagine any moral objection to Dolphin. Not that the poem, alas, from its donnée, can fail to wound.

Lowell appears wonderfully unaware that a poem that cannot fail to wound must have at least some moral objection to it. Anyway, the biography reports on these terrible debates and dilemmas without passing judgment, though at least one review that I have seen matches Auden's in righteous indignation.

The problem is not easily solved, nor does solution lie in some considered compromise between Auden's snooty evasions and Lowell's ruthless candor. Somehow Lowell must have clung to a fuddled conviction expressed in the line I have chosen for an epigraph: "Everything is real until it's published," whereupon, I think he may have felt, it becomes art, which is beyond the real but nearer the truth. Whatever theorizing or rationalizing may have lain behind this attitude, it took no account of the human pain it would engender. But Lowell's sense of the transformations wrought by art, removing its matter from the realm of the literal, is wonderfully documented. Jonathan Raban is quoted as observing that Lowell's revisions were usually a kind of gaming with words, treating them like billiard balls. For almost every sentence that Cal ever wrote if he thought it made a better line he'd have put a "never" or a "not" at the essential point. His favorite method of revision was simply to introduce a negative into a line, which absolutely reversed its meaning but very often would improve it. So that his poem on Flaubert ended with Flaubert dying, and in the first draft it went "Till the mania for phrases dried his heart"—a quotation from Flaubert's mother. Then Cal saw another possibility and it came out: "Till the mania for phrases enlarged his heart." It made perfectly good sense either way round, but the one did happen to mean the opposite of the other.

While it may be argued that there is considerable difference between tampering, on the one hand, with the words of Flaubert's mother, and, on the other, appropriating the most intimate domestic communications of an abandoned wife with whom the poet lived in great happiness for many years and who is the mother of his daughter, I think two other points must also be made. First, that any poet who habitually treats words and facts "like billiard balls" is likely to be convinced of their transmutability into a realm that is immune and indifferent to the literal. And, secondly, there is in this revision of the Flaubert poem an allegory of what Lowell must have felt about himself: if to others it appeared that his heart had dried, to the artist, to Lowell/Flaubert, it was clear that his heart was enlarged by the very act of finding words, by the very mania for phrases that so obsessed them both. It is a self-granted absolution of the sort Auden granted to Yeats, and to all who give life to language—in the first version of the final part of his famous elegy.

> Time that is intolerant
> Of the brave and innocent
>
> . . . .
>
> Worships language and forgives
> Everyone by whom it lives;
> Pardons cowardice, conceit,
> Lays its honors at their feet.

This is not a justification—the book is full of instances of Lowell's personal cruelty, attested to by Xandra Gowrie at some length and by Hardwick's declaration that at certain times for the poet "the deep underlying unreality is there, the fact that no one else's feelings really exist, . . ."—it is merely an attempt at an explanation.

In an address called "Fifty Years of American Poetry," delivered on October 22, 1962, at the Library of Congress's National Poetry Festival, Randall Jarrell said, "Lowell has always had an astonishing ambition, a willingness to learn what past poetry was and to compete with it on its own terms." This driving ambition and sense of competition was with him from the first and plays its role in other realms besides poetry. Hamilton quotes the first draft of "Waking in the Blue," then titled "To Ann Adden (Written during the first week of my voluntary stay at McLean's Mental Hospital)," from which these lines are taken:

> The bracelet on your right wrist jingles with
>   trophies:
> The enamelled Harvard pennant,
> the round medallion of St. Mark's School.
> I could claim both,
> for both were supplied by earlier,
> now defunct claimants,
> and my gold ring, almost half an inch wide,
> now crowns your bracelet, cock of the walk there.

And in a letter of tribute and admiration addressed to Theodore Roethke, Lowell says "I remember Edwin Muir arguing with me that there is no rivalry in poetry. Well, there is." This keenly competitive instinct accounts in some ways for his wholesale appropriations of The Western World's Great Poetry, all converted into what someone has called "Lo-Cal" in the volume called *Imitations*. But it also exhibits itself in somewhat more covert ways. For example, the most ambitious poem in *Lord Weary's Castle* is probably "The Quaker Graveyard in Nantucket." This poem is deservedly admired, studied, and commented upon by astute critics, who have located prose passages in Thoreau, as well as more conspicuous references from Melville, that are woven carefully into the fabric of the poem. It first appeared in what amount to two installments, in the Spring 1945 and Winter 1946 issues of *Partisan Review,* and longer by a great deal, when those two installments are assembled, than would appear in the final, careful pruning of the poem as the text we now know. Lowell's editing of his own poem was brilliant and right in every way; everything he eliminated was excessive and even sometimes rather shabby, and so it is not entirely out of order to wonder why such material had ever been included in the first place. The answer seems to me clear. If the two original installments are brought together, they come to one hundred and ninety-three lines of poetry, which is precisely the number of lines in "Lycidas."

In that chapter of Eileen Simpson's fine book of recollections, *Poets in Their Youth,* in which she focuses on Lowell, she records the matching excitement and enthusiasm both Lowell and John Berryman felt about Milton's poem. Describing a visit to Lowell and Jean Stafford in Maine, she writes:

> After Mass Jean repeated what she had said the previous evening; John and I mustn't think of leaving as originally planned. We must stay, Cal said. How could John even consider going when they hadn't discussed "Lycidas"? . . .
>
> The days of our visit, which stretched from a weekend to two weeks, fell into casual order. Although neither Cal nor John was supposedly working, there was never a time when they were not working. After breakfast and a good long recitation:
>
>> Bitter constraint, and sad occasion dear,
>> Compels me to disturb your season due;
>> For Lycidas is dead, dead ere his prime,
>
> and explication of "Lycidas," which they had no trouble agreeing was one of the greatest poems in the language (though there was the usual push/pull over the Three Greatest Lines), . . . Cal went up to his room.

A moment's reflection ought to make clear why this paradigm meant so much to Lowell when he came to write "The Quaker Graveyard." Here was one of the world's indisputably great poems, a marine elegy, formidable in its overt and hidden debts to its classical predecessors, distinguished for its striking outburst of moral indignation, the superlative work of a young but limitlessly ambitious poet, who not only composes a masterpiece but ends by announcing that he looks to even greater undertakings in "pastures new." As a model of substance, of congested and densely packed style, of concealed prophecy and covertly declared ambition, nothing could have served Lowell better.

But Milton, rebel and symbolic regicide, and "Lycidas," trumpet voluntary of independence and ambition disguised as a pastoral elegy, served Lowell in an even more intimate and psychologically far more important way, being bound up with his primal act of rebellion against his father, who had written a prudish and insinuating letter to the father of a girl young Lowell regarded as his fiancée. The letter was eventually turned over to the poet, who went home and knocked his father down, an event remembered again and again in a series of poems that have been examined with great sensitivity and understanding by David Kalstone in his book *Five Temperaments*. Hamilton furnishes two versions, one from *Notebooks 1967–68*, and the other an unpublished poem, written about 1956, and now in the Houghton Library at Harvard, from which these lines are taken:

> I hummed the adamantine
> ore rotundo of *Lycidas* to cool love's quarrels,
> and clear my honor
> from Father's branding Scarlet Letter. . . .
> "Yet once more, O ye laurels"—
> I was nineteen!

In his excellent chapter on Lowell, David Kalstone quotes Randall Jarrell thus: "If there were only some mechanism . . . for reasonably and systematically converting into poetry what we see and feel and are." That somewhat wistful yearning of Jarrell's took on the quality of a ravenous appetite in both Berryman and Lowell. And it is true that lyric poetry in our days has conceded vast territories to the writers of fiction, of which the impelling narrative drive is merely the most obvious advantage to the novelists. By its concentration, its narrowly focused point of view, its determined elimination of anything but the absolutely pertinent, its inviolably single tone, the lyric has elected to exclude all the contingent, chancy shifts of event, character, atmospherics, the alterations of time and consciousness that are the chief textures of our lives, and the vital substances of our very sense of reality. Novels are omnivorous, capable of assimilating everything, whereas the lyric has, since the Victorians, become more and more emaciated. Lowell's commendation of Elizabeth Bishop's volume *North & South and A Cold Spring* makes his own craving clear: "Her abundance of description reminds one, not of poets, poor symbolic, abstract creatures—but of the Russian novelists." And of Anne Sexton's first book he wrote, ". . . an almost Russian abundance and accuracy." Hamilton indicates how admiring and competitive Lowell felt about Berryman's *Dream Songs*, which were performing feats everyone assumed were denied to poetry. In Lowell's own words of 1964: "The Scene is contemporary and crowded with references to news items, world politics, travel, low-life, and Negro music. . . . By their impertinent piety, by jumping from thought to thought, mood to mood, and by saying anything that comes into the author's head, they are touching and nervously alive. . . . All is risk and variety here. This great Pierrot's universe is more tearful and funny than we can easily bear." And Frank Bidart, recalling Lowell as a teacher in the Spring 1977 issue of *Salmagundi*, a salute to Lowell's sixtieth birthday, writes, "One day in Robert Lowell's class, someone brought in a poem about a particularly painful and ugly subject. A student, who was shocked, said that some subjects simply couldn't be dealt with in poems. I've never forgotten Lowell's reply. He said, 'You can say anything in a poem—if you *place* it properly.'"

Out of this appetite and ambition came *Notebooks 1967–68*, reissued in 1970 in a "revised and expanded edition," and ultimately enlarged into *History* and *For Lizzie and Harriet*. From that vast richness I want to single out two versions of an unrhymed sonnet about Sir Thomas More:

> Hans Holbein's More, my friend since World War II,
> the gold chain of *S's*, the golden rose,
> the plush cap, the brow's damp feathertips of hair,
> the slate eyes' stern, facetious twinkle, ready
> to turn from executioner to martyr—
> or saunter with the great King's bluff arm on his neck,
> feeling that friend-slaying, terror-ridden heart
> beating under the fat of Aretino—
> some hanger-on saying, "How the King must love you!"
> And Thomas, "If it were a question of my head,
> or losing his meanest village in France . . ." Or standing
> below the scaffold and the two-edged sword—
> "Friend, help me up," he said, "when I come down,
> my head and body will shift for themselves."

This poem remained unaltered in the revised and enlarged edition of *Notebook* that came out in 1970. And for the moment I wish only to offer a guess that Aretino may have suggested himself because, besides being fat, like the King, and something of a womanizer, again like the King, and a poet, as the King was, too, his portrait by Titian hangs in New York's Frick Museum, directly across the room from Holbein's More.

> Holbein's More, my patron saint as convert,
> the gold chain of *S's*, the golden rose,
> the plush cap, the brow's damp feathertips of hair,
> the good eyes' stern, facetious twinkle, ready
> to turn from executioner to martyr—
> or saunter with the great King's bluff arm on your neck,
> feeling that friend-slaying, terror-dazzled heart
> ballooning off into its awful dream—
> a noble saying, "How the King must love you!"
> And you, "If it were a question of my head,
> or losing his meanest village in France. . . ."
> then by the scaffold and the headsman's axe—
> "Friend, give me your hand for the first step,
> as for coming down, I'll shift for myself."

This is the 1973 version from *History*. Before any comment on the differences, it may be worth remarking on the similarities, provided by Lowell's two main sources: the Holbein portrait and the first biography of More, written by his son-in-law, William Roper, the husband of More's favorite daughter, Margaret. Lowell makes use of two passages in Roper, which are worth quoting here.

> The King, allowing well his answer, said unto him: "It is not our meaning, Master More, to do you hurt, but to do you good would we be glad. We will therefore for this purpose [an arduous and dangerous embassy to Spain] devise upon some other, and employ your service otherwise." . . .
> And for the pleasure he took in his company would his grace suddenly sometimes come home to his house in Chelsea to be merry with him. Whither on a time, unlooked for, he came to dinner to him; and after dinner, in a fair garden of his, walked with him by the space of an hour, holding his arm about his neck.
> As soon as his grace was gone, I, rejoicing thereat, told Sir Thomas More how happy he was, whom the King had so familiarly entertained, as I never had seen him do to any other except Cardinal Wolsey, whom I saw his grace once walk with, arm in arm. "I thank our Lord, son," quoth he, "I find his grace my very good lord indeed; and I believe he doth as singularly favor me as any subject within this realm. Howbeit, son Roper, I may tell thee I have no cause to be proud thereof, for if my head could win him a castle in France (for then was there war between us) it should not fail to go."

And, later, this:

> And so was he by Master Lieutenant brought out of the Tower and from thence led towards the place of execution. Where, going up the scaffold, which was so weak that it was ready to fall, he said merrily to Master Lieutenant: "I pray you, Master Lieutenant, see me safe up and, for my coming down, let me shift for myself."

These passages are so well known, as is indeed the whole Roper text, that we may be astonished at some of the liberties Lowell has chosen to take, and a few I find either unfortunate or inexplicable. More's own terse, nearly jaunty gallows humor, being far more off-hand than either of Lowell's more cumbersome versions, is by just so much the more felicitous. And since Roper makes it clear that it was he himself who remarked with awe and joy upon the King's benevolent intimacy with More, made the observation directly to More himself, and he to whom More gave his shrewd reply, we must wonder why Lowell provided a nameless hanger-on in the first version, followed by a nameless noble in the second. I am not persuaded that he gains anything by either choice; instead, he loses a sense of the intimacy and candor of the statement: what one confesses, regarding the moral character of a monarch, to a family member one trusts will be quite different from what one might divulge to some courtier—and More was a prudent man.

What next puzzles is the retained line in which More is said to be "ready / to turn from executioner to martyr. . . ." Obviously, More has no executioner's part in Roper's biography; those accusations were raised against him by Foxe and later by Froude, among others. These charges have lately been revived by Jasper Ridley and Alistair Fox. What is strange, however, is to find them voiced by one who had chosen More as his patron saint, and who clearly knew More as the firm, mild-mannered, and compassionate man he is represented as being in Roper. And for this puzzle I will venture a conjectural answer.

With a sound instinct for drama and a self-lacerating honesty, Lowell identifies himself with both the king and the saint; and he is too cagey to reduce these wily antagonists into anything so allegorically simplified or so crudely doctrinal as The Good and The Bad. Opposed they are to one another, king and saint, but curiously alike in their divided inward selves. And not only do they resemble one another: in their determined opposition they are destined to enact the poet's personal torment. Fated by history to irreconcilable positions, they are also fated identities of the poet, More being able to be both intransigent fanatic and meek victim; Henry being able to be both benevolent patron and friend-slayer, whose "terror-dazzled heart" can go "ballooning off into its awful dream," presumably of lunatic omnipotence; the saint being able to "feel" the crazed heart of the king, in part, perhaps, because they are somehow alike, and are both linked to the poet, one by being his patron saint, the other by being like a famous licentious poet (now suppressed) as well as in other, more heart-rending and body-rending ways. The conversion of Roper's "castle" to "the meanest village" merely insists on Henry's ruthlessness, though it misses the overtones of a chess game, implied in More's comment. But the charges of no less ruthlessness against More are revived for the sake of the divided symmetries of the poem, which is terrifying in its awareness of the hideous cost of greatness. As for its relation to Lowell, Hamilton tells us, ". . . it always unnerved him to make enemies of friends."

Some years ago John Malcolm Brinnin had toyed with the idea of writing a biography of Lowell, and at that time he had a number of long talks with me. Once, he asked me point-blank whether I thought Lowell was in any way an anti-Semite, and after a moment's thought I answered flatly, "No." I would still answer that way now, though there are those who might feel entitled to think otherwise. Of Lowell's final lecture at the University of Cincinnati, when he was in perilous mental shape, Hamilton quotes Elizabeth Bettman as saying that he talked about "Hitler, more or less extolling the superman ideology. . . ." This was neither the beginning nor the end of Lowell's fascination with "great men" who were characterized by their "ruthlessness." But my own experiences with him were not only free of this particular dementia (though I was with him in several of his manic periods) but rather the reverse. Once, in his gentlest manner, Lowell asked me whether I was a believing Jew. For reasons that might not bear a too critical inspection, I said I was. He then said, "That means you think the Messiah is yet to come," and I assented. He asked whether I thought it might not be possible for the Messiah to be born, unrecognized, right in this country, and in our time. Given his pronounced excitement about the topic, together with my by now slightly informed sense of the symptoms of his illness, I was able to bring the whole conversation to a quiet conclusion by remarking that I thought it would be extremely difficult for any modern man to trace his ancestry irreproachably back to the House of David.

Writing of what we may call (if we disregard the early, privately printed, limited edition of *Land of Unlikeness*) Lowell's second book, *The Mills of the Kavanaughs*, Hamilton remarks, "It is immediately noticeable... that the book is a clamor of distraught, near-hysterical first-person speech, and that almost always the speaker is a woman. The men in the book are usually under attack. Thus, the rhetoric of 'Thanksgiving's Over' and of large sections of the title poem, can, not too fancifully, be heard as a fusing of two rhetorics—the enraged, erupting aggression of *Lord Weary* somehow loosened and given new spitefulness by echoes of letters Lowell had been getting—throughout 1947—from Jean Stafford, and echoes too (we might reasonably speculate) of the 'adder-tongued' invective that she used to pour into their quarrels."

As a description of the poem "Thanksgiving's Over," this is seriously off course and regrettable; and I am not concerned here with questions of biographical or autobiographical veracity, nor with the genesis or sources of Lowell's work. Instead, I want to indicate what strikes me, and furthermore, I would like to claim, must have struck Lowell himself, as a remarkable, over-arching design to his poetry, a thematic recapitulation or recurrence that resonates from the early work to the very latest with hollow and mordant overtones. It expresses itself, early and late, as a domestic drama of a bitter and terrifying kind, and early exhibits itself in "Thanksgiving's Over." The poem bears a headnote which reads,

> Thanksgiving night, 1942: a room on Third Avenue. Michael dreams of his wife, a German-American Catholic, who leapt from a window before she died in a sanatorium. The church is the Franciscan church on 31st Street.

Though the note says "Michael dreams" in the present tense, the whole poem is retrospectively cast in the past, giving it the sinister effect of a nightmare that cannot be exorcised or forgotten.

THANKSGIVING'S OVER*

Thanksgiving night: Third Avenue was dead;
My fowl was soupbones. Fathoms overhead,
Snow warred on the El's world in the blank snow.
"Michael," she whispered, "just a year ago,
Even the shoreleave from the *Normandie*
Were weary of Thanksgiving; but they'd stop
And lift their hats. I watched their arctics drop
Below the birdstoup of the Anthony
And Child who guarded our sodality
For lay-Franciscans, Michael, till I heard
The birds inside me, and I knew the Third
Person possessed me, for I was the bird
Of Paradise, the parrot whose absurd
Garblings are glory. *Cherry ripe, ripe, ripe . . .*"
Winter had come on horseback, and the snow,
Hostile and unattended, wrapped my feet
In sheepskins. Where I'd stumble from the street,
A red cement Saint Francis fed a row
Of toga'd boys with birds beneath a Child.
His candles flamed in tumblers, and He smiled.
"Romans!" she whispered, "look, these overblown
And bootless Brothers tell us we must go
Barefooted through the snow where birds recite:
Come unto us, our burden's light—light, light,
This burden that our marriage turned to stone!

---

*I have used here the greatly shortened form of the poem as it appears in *Selected Poems*. In its original form there was, admittedly, more vituperation, a good deal of it seemingly justified by dramatic context, on the part of the nameless and demented wife, who is the chief speaker of the poem. Her oscillations between hallucinatory piety and unbalanced acrimony offer not a little in the way of illustrating the poet's growing disenchantment with his adopted Roman Catholic faith. But for all the dead woman's tirades, as well as her craziness, the poem still follows the outline here presented.

> O Michael, must we join the deaf and dumb
> Breadline for children? Sit and listen." So
> I sat. I counted to ten thousand, wound
> My cowhorn beads from Dublin on my thumb,
> And ground them. *Miserere*? Not a sound.

There is enormous drama here and a complication of settings in time. Michael as dreamer or meditator sets the scene, but even as he does so it is in retrospect and chiefly in order to allow the remoter voice of his now dead wife to recall something still further in the past. She speaks reminiscently and, on the whole, reverently, though perhaps somewhat insanely with regard to her possession by the Holy Ghost, and with only a passing touch of bitterness or recrimination when mentioning "This burden that our marriage turned to stone!" though what is presented on the one hand as a touching and innocent piety is ironically undermined by an allusion to a Flaubert tale of credulous simplicity. Here the dead woman says,

> I heard
> The birds inside me, and I knew the Third
> Person possessed me, for I was the bird
> Of Paradise, the parrot whose absurd
> Garblings are glory. *Cherry ripe, ripe, ripe*. . . .

This confusion of parrot and Paraclete seems grotesquely to recall a similar confusion regarding a stuffed bird, a parrot, in Flaubert's *Un Coeur Simple* (A Simple Heart) and to remind us that the word "simple" is honorific in a religious context but contemptuous in a worldly one. The cry (*Cherry ripe, ripe, ripe*) is a well-known London street cry (weirdly echoed later in "our burden's light—light, light") which is also, in this poem, a bird cry, an especially apt conflation to suit St. Francis among the slums and gutters of lower Manhattan. Most of the poem is given to the patient, enduring, suffering voice of the dead woman, who concludes with a question and a plea:

> O Michael, must we join the deaf and dumb
> Breadline for children? Sit and listen. . . .

That request to Michael by his dead wife is not a request to listen to her. It is a plea to listen to the divine voice.

> So
> I sat. I counted to ten thousand, wound
> My cowhorn beads from Dublin on my thumb,
> And ground them. *Miserere?* Not a sound.

Divinity does not vouchsafe its voice to him, offers no mercy. And the only things that linger in the silence are the defunct syllables of anguish by a defunct wife. Though not explicitly accusatory, they are the words of one driven to madness and suicide, and they are also the words of one who can hear a divinity which to her husband is dumb. And possibly deaf. The poem leaves us wondering whether it is God or Michael who is unhearing. That muteness, that blank uncommunicative silence would reappear just as accusingly in poems Lowell wrote near the end of his career.

They are unrhymed sonnets, like the poem about Thomas More, and they appear, side by side, bearing the same title, in the volume called *For Lizzie and Harriet.* The poems are called "No Hearing," and they concern themselves with the pain and blankness that attends the end of love and marriage. Their common title seems worth a moment's consideration, not only because it bears upon that silence with which "Thanksgiving's Over" concludes, but because it appears twice as a refrain in George Herbert's penitential poem "Deniall." In considering the possibility of some connection, I mentioned the matter to the critic, David Kalstone, who replied as follows: "I think you're absolutely right about the Lowell poems. It isn't beyond him to repeat the title because it occurs twice in the Herbert poem. The 'silent universe our auditor' is, I suspect, an accidental glance at the 'silent ears' of 'Deniall.' But most of all it's the tone, the quoted, intervening voices . . . 'Skunk Hour' revisited in a more moving key . . . Cal knew Herbert very well. First on his own and then because Herbert was such a favorite of Elizabeth Bishop's. When EB left Castine [Lowell's home in Maine] after a troubled visit to the Lowells in 1957,

Cal gave her a two-volume family Herbert which had belonged to RTSL I [i.e., Lowell's grandfather]. 'Skunk Hour' [dedicated to Elizabeth Bishop] was written within a few weeks."

I want to quote the Herbert poem both for its beauty and its relevance.

DENIALL

When my devotions could not pierce
    Thy silent eares;
Then was my heart broken, as was my verse:
    My breast was full of fears
        And disorder:

My bent thoughts, like a brittle bow,
    Did flie asunder:
Each took his way; some would to pleasures go,
    Some to the wars and thunder
        Of alarms.

As good go anywhere, they say,
    As to benumme
Both knees and heart, in crying night and day,
    Come, come my God, O come,
        But no hearing.

O that thou shouldst give dust a tongue
    To crie to thee,
And then not heare it crying! all day long
    My heart was in my knee,
        But no hearing.

Therefore my soul lay out of sight,
    Untun'd, unstrung:
My feeble spirit, unable to look right,
    Like a nipt blossome, hung
        Discontented.

O cheer and tune my heartlesse breast,
    Deferre no time;
That so thy favours granting my request,
    They and my mind may chime,
        And mend my ryme.

The blankness of life, the bleak, heedless, unresponsive silence—these, in Lowell's poems are not relieved by even the possibility of prayer, and the disorder and dissolution of which they tell is worldly, secular, and irreparable. I have time this evening to attend only to the first of them.

NO HEARING

Belief in God is an inclination to listen,
but as we grow older and our freedom hardens,
we hardly even want to hear ourselves . . .
the silent universe our auditor—
I am to myself, and my trouble sings.
The Penobscot silvers to Bangor, the annual V
of geese beats above the moonborne bay—
their flight is too certain. Dante found this path
even before his first young leaves turned green;
exile gave seniority to his youth. . . .
White clapboards, black window, white clapboards, black
    window, white clapboards—
my house is empty. In our yard, the grass straggles. . . .
I stand face to face with lost Love—my breath
is life, the rough, the smooth, the bright, the drear.

This is a dense and rich poem about impoverishment, and its first line ("Belief in God is an inclination to listen") connects it intimately and directly with "Thanksgiving's Over" from a much earlier period in the poet's career. The poet here is able to acknowledge that "our freedom hardens" us and is itself imprisoning and isolating: "we hardly even want to hear ourselves . . . / the silent universe our auditor—" And then comes a line that appears in the text in italics: "*I am to myself, and my trouble sings.*" The line is at least a spiritual echo of details in "Skunk Hour" ("I hear / my ill-spirit sob in each blood cell"). But rendered conspicuous by being italicized, the line appears to declare itself a quotation or at least an allusion to some text outside Lowell's own corpus. I freely acknowledge that he may be quoting something I don't know and can't identify, but I'm prepared to make a wild guess nevertheless, and my guess is that this line is a parodic inversion of the refrain as it first appears in the first stanza of Spenser's "Epithalamion": "So I unto myselfe alone will sing, / The woods shall to me answer and my Eccho ring." Here, in Lowell's poem, which is the opposite of the marriage hymn Spenser composed for his own blissful marriage to Elizabeth Boyle, we have a line which is the reverse and negation of Spenser's, a grim and bitter finale: "I am to myself, and my trouble sings." The Penobscot River, the migrating geese, have their destinations and destinies, about which they have little or no choice. Dante's destiny, which involved his passage through Hell, was marked out for him when, at the age of nine, he fell in love with the only woman he would ever love, the Beatrice who would some day guide him to Paradise. Neither Dante, the river, nor the geese are as free as Lowell is, but they move to ends which are not only ordained but desirable. In contrast, Lowell sees his life and his future spelled out in black and white: "White clapboards, black window, white clapboards, black window, white clapboards—" a litany that ends with "my house is empty." And the poem ends with the same absence, the same solitariness that was dramatized in "Thanksgiving's Over." Here the poet says: "I stand face to face with lost Love—my breath / is life, the rough, the smooth, the bright, the drear." The poem becomes a small allegory at the end. Breath is indeed life for us all, but for Lowell it is also the allegory of the harsh, irreconcilable inconsistencies of life; the poor, run-of-the-mill, everyday infernos and paradisos that possess us like the random motions of atoms; the ordinary man's secular (rather than divine) comedy, which, unredeemed and unremarked by God, and played out beneath a heaven that is both deaf and dumb, seems for that very reason more like tragedy than comedy.

In one of his longest letters, composed on and off between February 14 and May 3, and written to George and Georgiana, his brother and sister-in-law in 1819, John Keats remarked:

> A Man's life of any worth is a continual allegory—and very few eyes can see the Mystery of his life—a life like the scriptures, figurative—which such people can no more make out than they can the hebrew Bible. Lord Byron cuts a figure—but he is not figurative—Shakespeare led a life of Allegory; his works are the comments on it—

If I began with a deceptively easy comparison of Lowell with Byron, I hope you will allow me to amend that judgment and to assert that if it is no more plausible to compare him with Shakespeare, he is, first of all, clearly and singularly, Robert Lowell—which, as a poet, is not a bad thing to be; and that through his constant moral and artistic endeavor to situate himself in the midst of our representative modern crises, both personal and political, he has led, for us—as it were, in our behalf—a life of Allegory; and his works are the comments on it.

OTHER PUBLICATIONS ON LITERATURE AVAILABLE FROM THE LIBRARY OF CONGRESS

The following publications, based on lectures presented at the Library of Congress, are available free from the Library of Congress, Central Services Division, Washington, D.C. 20540. When ordering, please specify the title, author, and date of publication.

CARL SANDBURG by Mark Van Doren. With a bibliography of Sandburg materials in the collections of the Library of Congress. 1969. 83 p.

CHAOS AND CONTROL IN POETRY, a lecture by Stephen Spender. 1966. 14 p.

THE INSTANT OF KNOWING by Josephine Jacobsen. 1974. 14 p.

JAMES JOYCE'S HUNDREDTH BIRTHDAY: SIDE AND FRONT VIEWS by Richard Ellmann. 1982. 33 p.

LITERARY LECTURES PRESENTED AT THE LIBRARY OF CONGRESS. 1973. 602 p.

LOUISE BOGAN: A WOMAN'S WORDS by William Jay Smith. With a bibliography. 1971. 81 p.

METAPHOR AS PURE ADVENTURE by James Dickey. 1968. 20 p.

PORTRAIT OF A POET: HANS CHRISTIAN ANDERSEN AND HIS FAIRYTALES by Erik Haugaard. 1973. 17 p.

RANDALL JARRELL by Karl Shapiro. With a bibliography of Jarrell materials in the collections of the Library of Congress. 1967. 47 p.

THE REASONS FOR POETRY AND THE REASON FOR CRITICISM by William Meredith. 1982. 36 p.

ROBERT FROST: LECTURES ON THE CENTENNIAL OF HIS BIRTH. 1975. 74 p. "In- and Outdoor Schooling: Robert Frost and the Classics" by Helen Bacon, "Toward the Source: The Self-Realization of Robert Frost, 1911-1912" by Peter Davison, "Robert Frost's 'Enigmatical Reserve': The Poet as Teacher and Preacher" by Robert Pack, "Inner Weather: Robert Frost as a Metaphysical Poet" by Allen Tate.

SAINT-JOHN PERSE: PRAISE AND PRESENCE by Pierre Emmanuel. With a bibliography. 1971. 82 p.

THE TRANSLATION OF POETRY. Address by Allen Tate and panel discussion presented at the International Poetry Festival held at the Library of Congress, April 13-15, 1970. 1972. 40 p.

TWO LECTURES. 1973. 31 p. "Leftovers: A CARE Package" by William Stafford and "From Anne to Marianne: Some Women in American Poetry" by Josephine Jacobsen.

WALLACE STEVENS: THE POETRY OF EARTH by A. Walton Litz. 1981. 15 p.

WALT WHITMAN: MAN, POET, PHILOSOPHER. 1955, reissued 1969. 53 p. "The Man" by Gay Wilson Allen, "The Poet" by Mark Van Doren, "The Philosopher" by David Daiches.